HOW DOES
CLOUD
COMPUTING
WORK?

Leon Gray

Please visit our website, www.garethstevens.com. For a free color catalog of all our high-quality books, call toll free 1-800-542-2595 or fax 1-877-542-2596.

Library of Congress Cataloging-in-Publication Data

Gray, Leon.

How does cloud computing work? / by Leon Gray.
  p. cm. — (High-tech science)
Includes index.
ISBN 978-1-4824-0392-3 (pbk.)
ISBN 978-1-4824-3309-8 (6-pack)
ISBN 978-1-4824-0391-6 (library binding)
1. Cloud computing. I. Gray, Leon, 1974-. II. Title.
TK5105.88813 G73 2014
004.6—dc23

First Edition

Published in 2014 by
Gareth Stevens Publishing
111 East 14th Street, Suite 349
New York, NY 10003

© 2014 Gareth Stevens Publishing

Produced by Calcium, www.calciumcreative.co.uk
Designed by Simon Borrough
Edited by Sarah Eason and Jennifer Sanderson

Photo credits: Cover: Shutterstock: Sukiyaki / Vladgrin. Inside: Dreamstime: Alexander Bedrin, Andrey Popov 27, Carrienelson1 21b, Danieloizo 34, Darren Baker 30, Dmyla 25b, Drserg 11t, Fabricio Rauen 23, Igor Mojzes 26, Kelvintt 20, 28, Lucien Milasan, 12, Manaemedia 22, Marin Conic 10, Pressureua 31, Sebast1an 33, Seemitch 3, 44, Shuttlecock 18b, Wavebreakmedia Ltd 29, Zhanna Malinina 38; Shutterstock: Ambrophoto 19, Andresr 35, Angela Waye 40, Blend Images 11b, Candace Hartley 8, D Hammonds, Dotshock 1, 13, Edyta Pawlowska 37, Franz Pfluegl 39t, JustinRossWard 45, NMedia, 14, Panom Pensawang 9, Pavel L Photo and Video 25t, PCruciatti 17, Pisaphotography 15, Pressmaster 43, 21t, Sashkin 24, 42, Seemitch 4, Shawn Hempel 7, Shebeko 36, Tim Jenner 6, Tommaso79 41, Tuulijumala 18t, ValeStock 39b; Wikimedia Commons: Ludovic Ferre 16.

Printed in the United States of America

CPSIA compliance information: Batch #CW14GS. For further information contact Gareth Stevens, New York, New York at 1-800-542-2595.

CONTENTS

CHAPTER ONE:
ALL IN THE CLOUD

Every day, hundreds of millions of people around the world use computer apps such as Dropbox, Gmail, iCloud, and Spotify. When people use these Internet-based services, they are making use of cloud computing, perhaps without knowing it!

Cloud computing connects PCs, laptops, smartphones, and tablets to services such as web mail and music on the Internet.

In the Cloud

Cloud computing is about using personal computers (PCs), laptops, Macs, smartphones, and other Internet-enabled electronic devices in new and exciting ways to unlock the power of the Internet.

Today, you can connect to cloud services on the move using a smartphone.

Defining the Cloud

In the world of information technology, cloud computing means providing services such as email and file storage to many users across a computer network. This is different from traditional desktop computing, where the apps people use and documents that they create are stored on a personal computer at home or in an IT suite at school.

Cloud for Business

For most businesses, the cloud is a private network within the company. The cloud is the internal network of servers and the services they provide. The server feeds into every computer terminal within the business so workers can access what they need.

Cloud for You

For most people, cloud computing is all the services they can plug into over the Internet. It places the apps and files we need on the Internet, making them available anywhere—at home, at school, or even out and about with a wireless connection and a tablet or Internet-enabled smartphone.

CLOUD SERVICES

Cloud computing covers many different web-based apps that people use every day. They include web mail such as Gmail and Hotmail, file storage systems such as Dropbox, social networking sites such as Facebook and Twitter, and music clouds such as iTunes and Spotify.

CLOUD CHANGES

Cloud computing is changing the way we use computers. Instead of running all the programs on a computer at home, cloud computing uses remote machines in the "cloud" to run them for you.

Babbage never made his Analytical Engine. However, in 1991, scientists from the London Science Museum built a replica from Babbage's drawings to prove that it worked.

The Computer Age

Cloud computing would not be possible without the development of personal computing. In 1882, English mathematician Charles Babbage designed the first computer. His steam-powered machine, named the Analytical Engine, could add up tables of numbers.

The Electronic Age

In 1943, British mathematician Alan Turing built Colossus, the first fully electronic computer. Colossus was designed to crack secret codes used by the Germans during World War II (1939–1945).

Three years later, US physicists John Atansoff, John Mauchly, and Presper Eckert built the Electronic Numerical Integrator and Calculator (ENIAC). The enormous machine weighed an incredible 30 tons (27 mt).

Microchips are the "brains" of modern computers. These tiny chips do all the complex calculations to run different tasks, such as open an app or print a document.

Integrated Circuits and Microchips

Computers became much smaller following the invention of the transistor in 1947. Scientists realized they could build all the electronic parts of a computer on one small circuit board, called an integrated circuit (IC). This led to the invention of the microprocessor, or microchip. Microchips made computers much smaller and more powerful.

Personal Computers

During the 1970s, the first PCs were invented. Computer experts developed operating systems for people to use the new PCs, such as Microsoft's MS-DOS and Apple's Graphical User Interface (GUI). At the same time, they developed programs, such as word processing and spreadsheets.

COMPUTER AGE

The first laptop computers appeared in the 1980s. Apple's iMac revolutionized desktop computing when it appeared in the 1990s. Today, computers exist in many different forms, from netbooks and smartphones to tablets and smart televisions.

COMPUTER TALK

The computing revolution meant that more people owned computers. The next logical step was making PCs "talk" to each other so people could use them to share data and communicate with each other.

Sharing Data

Before the computing revolution, people had to physically share computers to access the data on another computer. So computer experts came up with inventions, such as floppy disks, to make sharing data much easier and more practical for people.

Before cloud computing, people used floppy disks to store and share data. These disks stored data as a pattern of magnetic particles on a thin plastic film.

Early Networks

In 1962, Joseph Linklider came up with the idea of a computer network while working at the Advanced Research Projects Agency (ARPA). He called his idea the Intergalactic Computer Network. It worked using a new communication protocol called packet switching—transferring messages as neat packets of data. Eventually, this developed into the Advanced Research Projects Agency Network (ARPANET for short). ARPANET paved the way for the Internet.

These colored Ethernet cables connect all the computers in a LAN in a busy office.

Ethernet

In 1973, Robert Metcalfe developed Ethernet. Ethernet could be used to connect many computers and other devices within a building. Ethernet worked by using cables running from machine to machine in a local area network (LAN).

Bigger Networks

Computer networks can be much bigger than a LAN. Metropolitan area networks (MANs) connect computers in whole towns or cities using telephone lines. Bigger still are wide area networks (WANs), which can cover almost any geographical area. The Internet is an example of a WAN.

WIRELESS NETWORKS

Today, people in offices and at home connect to devices, such as printers, using wireless networking (WiFi) technology. Instead of using cables, WiFi uses radio waves to transmit data through the network.

SUPER SHARING

The Internet is a WAN that covers the entire planet. In reality, it is a global "network of networks" through which people can share ideas and information, and communicate with each other.

Internet Origins

The Internet started in the early 1960s, when scientists from the United States Defense Department set up a computer network called Advanced Research Projects Agency Network (ARPANET). They invented the language that allowed computers to share information and communicate, making the Internet possible.

People make use of cloud computing every time they check email or post a message on Facebook or Twitter.

Supercomputers

At first, the network consisted of just three computers based at universities in the United States. By 1984, more than 1,000 computers were connected to ARPANET. In 1986, the National Science Foundation (NSF) set up five supercomputing centers to speed up the connections to ARPANET. Within a year, the number of computers connected to the network had grown to 10,000. Eventually, the new NSF network (NSFNET) replaced ARPANET to become the backbone of the Internet in the United States.

Berners-Lee created the World Wide Web while he was working at the European Laboratory for Particle Physics (CERN).

In 2012, Americans spent more than $185 billion shopping on the Internet.

Global Network

By the 1990s, the Internet had expanded throughout the world. Companies called Internet Service Providers (ISPs) started to sell Internet access to individual users. Then, in 1991, British computer scientist Tim Berners-Lee developed the World Wide Web. This invention allowed people to use web pages stored on servers connected to the Internet.

MODERN INTERNET

In 1995, the NSF handed over management of the Internet to the ever-growing number of ISPs. Today, the Internet connects people in more than 65 countries around the world. It helps people keep up-to-date with the news, play games, buy groceries or theater tickets, and chat with family and friends nearby or far away.

END TO END

Cloud computing is divided into the front (user) end and the back (system) end. The front and back ends communicate with each other through a computer network, which is most often the Internet.

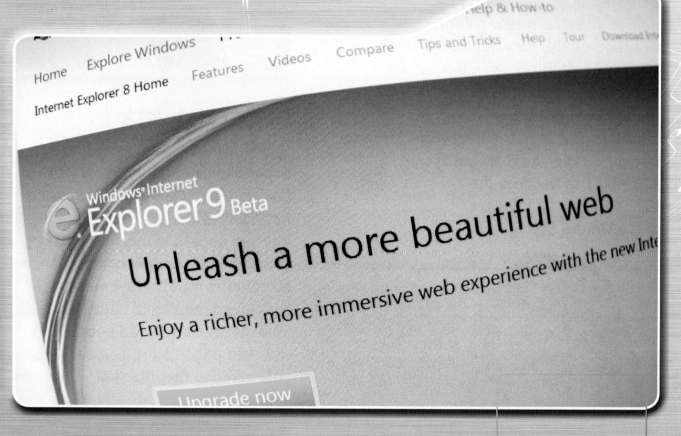

Front End

The front end of a cloud computing system is the part that the computer user actually uses. It includes the user's personal computer and/or computer network and the interface software. Interface software is needed to access the cloud computing system.

Many cloud services, such as web-based email (Gmail and Hotmail), use Internet browsers such as Internet Explorer or Google Chrome. Other cloud computing systems, such as the music cloud Spotify, have their own apps that provide users with access to the cloud services.

Most people interact with cloud services using a web browser such as Microsoft's Internet Explorer.

Back End

The back end is the "cloud" section of the system. This includes all the various computers, servers, and file storage systems that make up the cloud of computing services. Cloud services include almost every type of app, from email and file storage to music and video games. In most cases, each app will have its own dedicated server.

Follow the Rules

The front and back end of a cloud computing system use computer software, called middleware, to "speak" to each other. A central server administers the cloud system and follows a specific set of rules, called protocols, to ensure everything runs smoothly.

The cloud is all the computers, servers, and other equipment working behind the scenes to provide web mail, file storage, and other services.

WHAT'S IN A NAME?

Cloud computing gets its name because all the applications and information exist on a cloud of web servers rather than on the individual user's workstation.

CHAPTER TWO

THE INTERNET

The Internet is the backbone of most cloud computing systems. The only thing you need to run cloud services is the interface software, which is usually a web browser.

Internet Protocol

When scientists started the Internet, they needed to allow computers to share data in a way that made sense to everyone. They set up rules so that all the computers on the network followed the same set of instructions. This set of rules became known as the TCP/IP Suite—the Transmission Control Protocol (TCP) and Internet Protocol (IP).

Data Packets

Using the TCP/IP Suite, any information to be transferred through the network is broken down into smaller parts called "packets." Each packet is given an Internet Protocol (IP) address, which is a special number for the destination computer.

Billions of people use the World Wide Web to find information on the Internet. You need a web browser to display this information for you.

Data Switch

As the data packet passes through the computer network toward its destination, file servers "switch" the packet along the way. The IP address of the packet tells the servers which way to switch the packet. Each time a server switches the packet, it gives the packet a "wrapper." This tells us which and how many servers handled the packet on its journey.

Information Highway

Data packets from the same computer file do not always travel along the same route, but they all end up at the same destination. Imagine the network as the highways and roads. A group of ten people (packets) cannot fit in one car, so they are more likely to get to their destination if they split up. Each person will travel in a different vehicle and maybe along different roads, but they will all end up at the same destination.

Protocols route information through the Internet in a way that shows the path of each piece of data from the start of its journey to its end.

SUPER SWITCH

A file sent from the United States to Australia can be switched up to 15 times. This means 15 file servers were needed to deliver the packet to its destination.

ROUTING AROUND

Different organizations work together to exchange information over the Internet. Most people pay an ISP to use Internet services. In turn, the ISP pays bigger organizations higher up the chain.

Tier 3 Networks

The Internet uses many different ISPs to route information. Consumers are at the bottom of the chain. They include individual computer users and businesses, which pay a fee to an ISP to connect to the Internet. The ISP is the first step in the routing hierarchy. All the ISPs together make up what is known as a Tier 3 network.

This diagram shows how an ISP in a Tier 3 network is connected to a Tier 1 network so that information can be routed around the Internet.

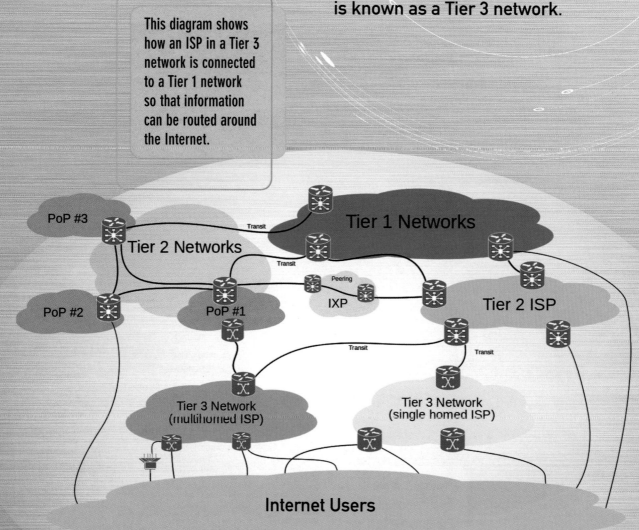

PoP #3

Tier 1 Networks

Transit

Tier 2 Networks

Transit

Peering

PoP #2

IXP

PoP #1

Tier 2 ISP

Transit

Transit

Tier 3 Network
(multihomed ISP)

Tier 3 Network
(single homed ISP)

Internet Users

More than 570 million people in China connect to the Internet regularly. Cloud services such as social networking and online video sharing are among the most popular online activities.

Tier 2 Networks

All the ISPs on the Tier 3 network pay to connect to one or more ISPs on the Tier 2 network. ISPs on the Tier 2 network are Internet providers. All the ISPs on a Tier 2 network pay to connect to a Tier 1 network. Some also use "peering." Peering means the ISPs on the Tier 2 network share each other's Internet traffic for free. Peering opens up more connections to the Internet. It also allows for more information sharing and improves the performance of each ISP.

Tier 1 Networks

Tier 1 networks are made up of enormous telecommunications companies, all of which share Internet traffic with each other without paying for the service. Historically, ARPANET and later NSFNET made up the Tier 1 network. Big telecommunications companies took over when the US government opened up the Internet to the public in 1995.

ACCESS ALL AREAS

In the past, people needed a desktop computer, a modem, and a telephone line to use the Internet. Today, using a wireless connection to devices such as tablets and smartphones, you can access the Internet from just about anywhere in the world.

New Rules

Before the Web was created, most Internet users were computer experts. Most people could not understand the complex language and tools needed to share information on the Internet. In 1991, Tim Berners-Lee created five new ways to transfer information through the Internet. These protocols, which are still used today, are: HTTP (HyperText Transfer Protocol), FTP (File Transfer Protocol), POP (Post Office Protocol), SMTP (Simple Mail Transfer Protocol), and NNTP (Network News Transfer Protocol).

Devices called routers ensure information ends up in the right place. This could be a file sent between two people in an office or an email sent halfway around the world.

Without the HyperText Transfer Protocol, viewing web pages on a computer or tablet using an Internet browser would be impossible.

User Friendly

The five new protocols became known as the W3 protocols, named for the W3 Consortium that was set up to oversee the development of the Internet. Today, anyone can use the Internet to access and share thoughts and information. People use web browsers to find and read web pages using the HTTP protocol. FTP clients allow people to share and download files using the FTP protocol. Email programs use the POP and SMTP protocols. NNTP is used to exchange messages, called articles or posts, between users on Internet discussion forums.

Digital Revolution

Today, more than 2.5 billion people regularly use Internet services such as the World Wide Web and email. The Internet allows us to keep in touch with family and friends, make new friends on social networking sites, go shopping, play games, learn new skills, and find out about almost anything.

MOBILE INTERNET

Mobile access is one of the fastest-growing areas of the Internet. Anyone with a smartphone and a wireless connection can access services such as email and the World Wide Web. Cloud computing is an important part of this mobile revolution, because it allows people to access important files and services wherever they are.

Many people use mobile devices such as smartphones to access cloud services such as web mail.

CHAPTER THREE:
IN THE CLOUD

Most people are familiar with the front end of a cloud computing service. This is usually a website or an app that they use to access files, play music, or post a status update. The back end is the invisible part you cannot see. This is where all the processing takes place and where the cloud exists.

Server Basics

Imagine a data center humming with racks of machines called servers. When you log on to a cloud service, you are plugging into these powerful computers. Some servers give commands to allow you to do specific tasks, such as log on to an account or play a music file. Other servers are simply massive storage drives that hold important files. Together, these servers become a cloud of resources.

When you log on to iTunes, you are connecting to Apple's massive servers to access music files from the cloud.

Local Servers

A server is any computer and the software on the computer that is used to manage resources on a network. In a LAN in an office, there may be a file server to store important files. Any computer on the office network can access the files through the file server. An office network might also have a print server so any computer can print to a networked printer.

Most offices use a server as the backbone of a LAN. The network allows workers to share and store files.

You can find out more information about Justin Bieber by logging on to his personal website.

Web Servers

The Internet relies on web servers to deliver web pages to computers connected to the Web. To do this, the computer uses a computer program called a browser. The browser sends a request to the web server in the form of a uniform resource locator (URL). A URL consists of three main parts: the HTTP protocol, the server name, and the file name. Look at the following URL: http:/www.justinbiebermusic.com/believecharity

- HTTP is the HyperText Transfer Protocol—the language that the browser uses to find and speak to the web server.

- www.justinbiebermusic.com identifies the Justin Bieber web server name.

- believecharity is the file name for Justin Bieber's charity drive.

The server then processes the request to deliver the page back to your web browser, so you can read Justin Bieber's charity page.

SERVERS IN THE CLOUD

Most cloud systems rely on several servers to deliver their services. Web servers handle the requests to connect and relay data between a user and the server. File servers store data such as documents and music files. All these servers work together to deliver the cloud service.

VIRTUAL SERVERS

Some cloud services have millions of registered users, so they need a lot of servers to do lots of different jobs. One way to manage this is to create "virtual" servers, which increase the power of the service so it can handle many tasks, without needing to buy extra computer hardware.

Increasing Capacity

Most servers usually do one particular task. This streamlines the computer network and makes it easier to solve problems. However, as a computer network grows, more servers are needed to carry out an increasing number of tasks. The additional servers take up a lot of room and generate a lot of heat. "Virtualization" can solve these problems.

Hosts and Guests

Virtualization involves using one computer to "host" a virtual server. Instead of functioning as part of the computer, the virtual server behaves like a completely separate device. For example, a computer running the Microsoft Windows operating system could be used to host a virtual server that runs another operating system, such as Linux. The computer is called the host machine, and the virtual server is the guest. While the host computer runs all the Windows apps, the virtual server can run the apps for the Linux system. The two systems do different jobs on the same computer.

Smartphones run a single operating system (OS). Virtualization allows devices to run more than one OS, so they can perform multiple tasks.

```
MS-DOS version 1.25
Copyright 1981,82 Computer, Inc.

Command v. 1.1
Current date is Tue 1-01-1980
Enter new date:
Current time is 1:01:56.20
Enter new time:

A:
```

In the past, most PCs worked using Microsoft Disk Operating System (MS DOS). Modern PCs can run more than just one operating system, creating a virtual machine that performs many different tasks.

WORLD'S FIRST

Computer scientists working at IBM (International Business Machines) created the world's first virtual computer in the 1960s. The experimental system was built on the IBM 7044 computer, which hosted multiple 7044 guest machines.

Virtual Benefits

Virtual servers can run several tasks on one physical machine. Since fewer machines are needed, using a virtual server saves energy and avoids the need to buy more expensive hardware. Virtualization also reduces maintenance costs—it is much quicker and easier to update just one computer running multiple virtual servers than it is to maintain several individual computers.

SUPER SERVICE

Multitenancy is one of the buzz words of cloud computing. This is where one server carries out all the different tasks needed to run the service, and serves every single customer.

Racks of cloned servers provide the processing power to enable cloud services such as DropBox and iCloud.

Computer Clones

In an office, one server handles requests from all the computers on the network. In the cloud, a single server may serve millions of customers. One physical server would not be able to deal with all these requests alone. As a result, many cloud systems use multitenancy. This means there are several identical servers (clones) to handle all the traffic. Every one of these servers is exactly the same. Users can connect to any one of these cloned machines and it will be able to deal with their request.

Multitenancy ensures people can access cloud services 24 hours a day, wherever they are.

Benefits

Many popular cloud services, such as Dropbox, iCloud, Google Apps, and Netsuite, work using the multitenancy model of cloud computing. One of the main benefits of multitenancy cloud computing is that if one server fails, all the information is safely stored on all the other clones, so users can access information all the time.

LOAD BALANCING

Multitenancy increases the speed of cloud services, regardless of how many people are using them. Imagine a web mail service such as Gmail with millions of users. Multitenancy ensures that the service can handle all the traffic if everyone sent an email at the same time. Servers called load balancers handle the peaks and troughs of demand. These servers direct all the messages to the right place as soon as they are sent. This ensures a speedy service for everyone.

iCloud

The iCloud is Apple Computer's suite of cloud services, which includes web mail and file storage.

AT YOUR SERVICE

Cloud service providers offer three basic services: Software as a Service (SaaS), Platform as a Service (PaaS), and Infrastructure as a Service (IaaS).

Software as a Service

SaaS delivers one app to several customers. The provider owns the app and uses the Internet to deliver the service through a web browser, a dedicated app, or both. Customers benefit because there is no software to purchase, install, and update—the service provider does all of this for him or her. One example of a cloud-based SaaS app is Google's Gmail. This webmail service replaces traditional desktop email clients such as Microsoft Outlook.

Platform as a Service

PaaS allows customers to send apps to people via the Internet. In this case, the customer is a business that develops its own customized apps. The service provider provides hardware, software, and hosting services to deliver web-based apps. An example of a cloud platform is Force.com, which hosts cloud services for many external customers.

When you sign up for most cloud services, you download the software you need to use it. You can also access the service using a web browser.

Cloud services such as Skype run on the CaaS model. Skype offers Internet phone calls, instant messaging, and video conferencing services to users.

Infrastructure as a Service

Some companies, such as Amazon and Google, hire out the computing resources to host cloud services. They provide all the hardware, such as servers, networking, and a data center, so other companies can provide the service. This is called Infrastructure as a Service (IaaS). One example is Netflix, which streams movies and television programs to customers using Amazon's cloud platform.

NEW MODELS

Two new types of cloud computing include Network as a Service (NaaS) and Communication as a Service (CaaS). NaaS delivers network services, such as servers and routing equipment, to customers over the Internet. CaaS provides cloud-based services such as phone calls and video conferencing.

27

CLOUDS FOR EVERYONE

Cloud computing can be offered to different customers in different ways. These are called deployment models and they control who is allowed to use the cloud services. There are three main deployment models: public clouds, private clouds, and hybrid clouds.

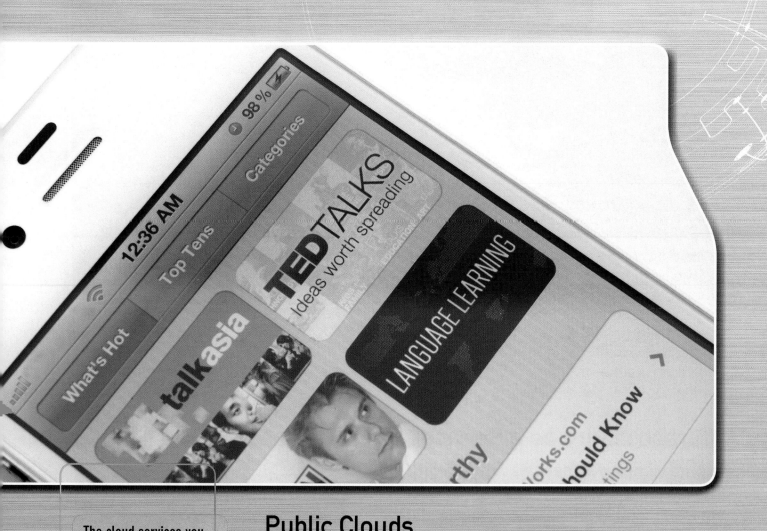

The cloud services you can access via apps or Internet browsers on your smartphone are public clouds.

Public Clouds

Public clouds give people quick access to the resources needed to use a cloud service. The service provider manages the hardware, software, and supporting infrastructure, and offers cloud services such as apps and file storage to the general public. Many public clouds are free, although some charge a fee. Most public clouds offer people access through the Internet via a browser or app interface.

Some companies run private cloud services that are available only to their employees and clients.

THE INTERCLOUD

One exciting new idea in cloud computing is to combine all the different cloud services into one huge cloud network, called the "Intercloud." This global "cloud of clouds" would be similar to the Internet, the global "network of networks" on which most cloud services are based.

Private Clouds

Some companies run private cloud services that limit the cloud service to one company. Private clouds usually use the PaaS model (see page 26). The company develops the software and then uses it through an external service provider. In this way, companies can deliver specific software to employees and clients without the infrastructure costs. Private cloud companies also have control over the service, which keeps the data safe.

Hybrid Clouds

Hybrid clouds are based on private clouds. However, they also take advantage of the benefits of public clouds. Companies may use private clouds for applications and sensitive data, but still rely on the benefits of public cloud services, such as hardware and software support.

CHAPTER FOUR:
CLOUD SERVICES

Cloud computing provides access to email and all our important documents from anywhere, from any device, and at any time. Cloud computing is all about being connected. It is the perfect partner to our mobile lives.

Mobile devices provide users with instant access to cloud services such as web mail.

Email Accounts

Web mail services allow people to send and receive emails through a website. The website can be accessed using a web browser.

A POP (Post Office Protocol) account allows messages to be sent and received using an email client, or program, such as Microsoft's Outlook Express. Every time you check your email, the account downloads your new messages from the mail server into the email program.

IMAP (Internet Message Access Protocol) accounts also allow people to send and receive emails using an email program. However in these accounts, the messages are stored in the cloud rather than by the email program.

Take Advantage

Web mail offers many advantages over desktop email clients. For example, web mail services offer so much online storage that you can leave all your emails and attachments in the cloud. You can then access them from anywhere and download them to an email program on your PC if you wish.

Web Mail Drawbacks

One of the downsides of web mail is that you will have to see advertisements when viewing your messages on the web. Although most web mail services are currently free of charge, there is always the chance that you might have to start paying for them in the future.

Tablet devices such as Apple's iPad allow easy access to cloud services such as Skype video conferencing.

SKYPE

The Internet has also provided new ways of communicating with people through cloud services that offer phone calls and video conferencing over the Internet. One of the most popular is Skype, which was launched in 2003.

STORING FILES

Many people struggle to find enough storage space to store all their digital photos, MP3 files, and video clips. Some people store these important files on external hard drives, compact discs, and flash devices. Cloud storage is now a popular alternative.

Storage Solutions

There are many different ways that you can store important documents in the cloud. They are all available anywhere that you can connect to the Internet. Hosting companies store the files on remote servers in large data centers. People can access their data using an app or through a regular web browser.

Cloud storage offers 24-hour access to all your important documents and files.

Apple's iDisk

Today, the iDisk is one of the most popular cloud-based storage solutions. This iDisk service comes as part of Apple's iCloud subscription. The Mac's operating system creates an icon of the iDisk on your desktop. All you need to do is copy the files that you want to store in the cloud. The Mac then synchronizes all the files in the iDisk on your Mac to the cloud's web servers. iDisk also allows users to synchronize files onto more than one computer. This means you can work on a document at school and an up-to-date version of the file will be waiting on your Mac at home. iDisk also has a public folder, so users can share files that are too big to be sent as email attachments.

Most cloud storage services offer password protection to keep your private documents safe.

SAFETY CONCERNS

One of the main concerns people have with cloud storage solutions is the security of the data. Any information that is stored in the cloud is vulnerable to unauthorized access. Fortunately, most cloud services use techniques, such as password protection, to ensure the information stays private.

Dropbox

Another popular file-hosting service is Dropbox. Users create a special folder on each device they own, and the Dropbox service synchronizes it so the folder that appears is same on every device. Users can also upload files using a web browser, or use an app to access the service.

SOCIAL CLOUDS

Social networking sites are changing the way people use the Internet. These popular sites are helping people to stay in touch, make new friends, post comments, upload photos, and even more. These sites are forms of cloud storage.

Twitter is one of the most popular social networking sites. It allows people to share information via tweets.

Social Success

Facebook and Twitter are two of the most popular social networking sites. Facebook has been around since 2004 and already boasts more than one billion active users worldwide. Twitter came later in 2006 and has 500 million registered users.

TWITTER

Twitter allows users to post short 140-character messages called "tweets" to tell other Twitter users what they are thinking or doing. Twitter is an open site so you can follow any other user. When someone whom you are following posts a tweet, the message appears in your Twitter feed.

Keeping in Touch Via the Cloud

Social media sites are excellent types of cloud computing services. Sites such as Facebook, Giant Hello, and Beebo allow people to develop real relationships within the virtual world of the Internet. People can keep in touch with family and friends using messaging systems, chat forums, and blogging tools, which can be used to post "status updates" and send out invitations to events. Many sites also allow users to upload photos and tag people who feature in the images. All the information people post on their profiles is stored in the cloud so it can be accessed whenever they want.

MUSIC CLOUDS

Cloud computing has changed the way people listen to music. In the past, to listen to music, compact discs and, later, MP3 files were played. Cloud music services use computer servers connected to the Internet to let people access an enormous library of digital music files.

Music Match

Some music clouds, such as Pandora, are like personalized radio stations. Users create a profile and build up a library of music. Pandora then streams music over the Internet to match your music tastes. You can approve or reject the songs that Pandora selects, and the service automatically revises the playlist. Music clouds such as Spotify offer users more control over the music they hear. Users can search through Spotify's library of music, adding specific songs to make up personalized playlists of their favorite music.

Compact discs have become less popular as more people listen to music on cloud services such as Pandora and Spotify.

PREMIUM ACCOUNTS

Most music clouds have a version that you can try for free. They offer basic accounts with the minimum storage space and may include advertisements between songs. Premium accounts offer extra services, such as more storage space and streaming to mobile devices, but you must pay for them.

Uploading Music

iTunes and Amazon Cloud Player work in a different way. Users can upload their own digital music files and the service stores the files in an online music library. Users can then play the music from the website or using the service's desktop or smartphone app. These services also allow people to purchase new music and add the digital files to their playlists.

File Storage

Music clouds that work as a file storage service usually limit the number of songs you can save in your online library. For example, Amazon Cloud Player gives you 5 gigabytes of free storage space, which can hold around 1,000 songs.

CHAPTER FIVE

PROS AND CONS

Cloud computing has its advantages and disadvantages. When you use cloud services such as web mail and social networks, you have to balance the benefits against the risks.

Cloud Benefits

There are many different reasons why so many people are moving toward cloud computing. One of the main benefits is ease of access. Many people rely on cloud services instead of a desktop computer to access apps and important files. Most cloud services work using the Internet, which is available almost anywhere in the world at any time.

Cutting the Cost

Cloud computing reduces the need for costly computer equipment and all the hardware that goes with it. You need just a simple Internet-enabled device, such as a smartphone or tablet, and a WiFi connection. The service provider pays for all the costly hardware, software licenses, and maintenance costs and IT support.

Free WiFi access cuts the cost of accessing cloud services such as web mail.

You can listen to your favorite artists in the cloud, and then purchase tickets to see them live in concert.

Saving Space

Hosting servers takes up a lot of space. Some companies rent rooms to store all this equipment because they do not have enough space on site. Cloud computing now gives users the option of storing the data in a remote site. Remote data centers also offer added benefits, such as security and regular server backups.

Ticketing companies have reaped the benefits of cloud computing, speeding up ticket sales for music fans.

PROCESSING POWER

Cloud services offer increased server capacity to handle lots of traffic. Imagine a ticketing company that sells tickets for a popular artist. Cloud services can tap into the processing power of many computers, speeding up the ticket sales.

CLOUD CONCERNS

The idea of handing over important information to a service provider to host on the Internet raises concerns. The biggest worries are privacy and security as well as reliability.

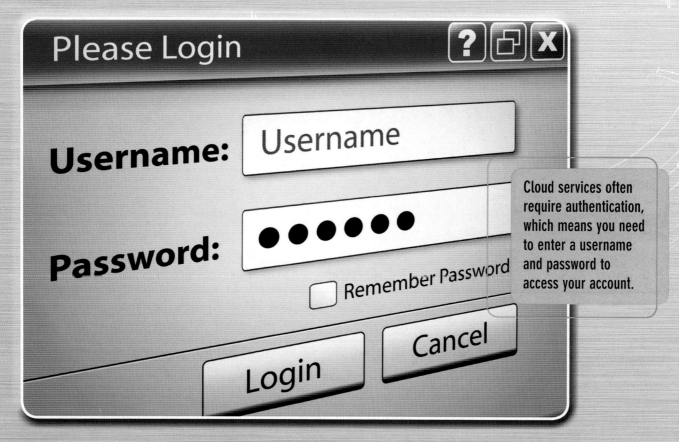

Please Login

Username: Username

Password: ●●●●●●

☐ Remember Password

Login   Cancel

Cloud services often require authentication, which means you need to enter a username and password to access your account.

Security and Privacy

If you can access all your important computer files in the cloud, there is always the risk that someone else could access them, too, and use them without your knowledge. As a result, almost all cloud service providers use different authentication and authorization processes to protect data in the cloud.

Authentication protects data using a password. Users create their own passwords when they sign up to the service. The data itself is also encrypted, which means it is scrambled up and requires an encryption key to decode. You unlock the encryption key by entering the correct password. Authorization involves giving specific users access to apps and files, which can be restricted by profile. Each user can then access only the data and apps relevant to his or her profile.

Reliability

Most people take cloud computing for granted, but what happens if something goes wrong? Do you want to store important data if the cloud is going to fail? Internet connections are not always reliable, and technical problems will occur from time to time. On Christmas Eve 2012, Amazon cloud services went offline following a technical glitch caused by a human error. Amazon cloud services were unavailable for more than 22 hours, resulting in a huge loss of cash for sites relying on Christmas revenue.

DATA OWNERSHIP

Another problem faced by users of cloud computing is the ownership of data. If you give another company your personal information, do you still own the data? When you sign up for cloud services, you must agree to the terms and conditions of the sites. It is important to read these legally binding documents carefully before you agree to use the services.

Most cloud services have privacy settings to keep your private information safe from cybercriminals.

LOOK TO THE CLOUDS

Cloud computing is not just about moving servers into a data center. It is changing the way people use computers to store data and access services such as music and social networks.

Behind the scenes, racks of computer servers provide the processing power to offer services such as web mail, file storage, and music clouds.

Hiding in the Cloud

Cloud computing is everywhere. These services are hidden behind the Internet so many people are not aware of the cloud, even though they rely on it to go about their work or for fun. Cloud computing is revolutionizing the way people use computers and the Internet. It is helping them tackle the challenges of computer upgrades, maintenance, and security.

Using the Cloud

Many people now use cloud services to store important information, such as photos, which take up a lot of memory. Schools, companies, and universities rely on cloud computing to store apps and libraries of information. Games such as Minecraft are also using cloud services. They allow many users to create "servers" to play with other users, making games more interactive.

Future Trends

Cloud computing may seem like the next trend in personal computing, but it is not an end in itself. Cloud computing is a helpful technology. It is helping individuals and companies to achieve their goals and making computing much easier for everyone to use. Cloud services such as iTunes and iCloud have come a long way in such a short space of time. Who knows what the future may hold in store?

The cloud is an online "library" of services that provides us with access to a range of different information.

CLOUDS ALL AROUND US

Cloud computing has been around for many years, but it seems to be the new buzz phrase in information technology. Web mail, social networking, and cloud storage are some of the most popular applications of cloud computing, and it looks like that trend will continue.

Internet Access

Most cloud computing systems make use of the Internet to provide their services to many users around the world. They have developed smart tools such as virtualization and multitenancy to ensure people can access the cloud from anywhere in the world at all times.

Cloud Services

Many companies now offer cloud services. They include web mail services such as Gmail and Outlook, file sharing apps such as SendSpace and Dropbox, social networks such as Facebook and Twitter, and music clouds such as iTunes and Spotify.

Many people access cloud services on their smartphones without even realizing it.

WiFi access and mobile devices are making it much easier to access cloud services.

Advantages and Disadvantages

Cloud services have advantages and disadvantages. Some of the advantages include easy access, increased processing power, and reduced hardware costs. Some of the disadvantages include concerns about privacy and security and issues surrounding ownership of the data in the cloud.

Cloud Future

More people are turning away from traditional desktop computers in favor of mobile computing. They are using Internet-enabled devices such as smartphones and tablets. The future of cloud services looks set to continue.

CLOUD CONFIDENCE

The confidence in cloud computing is growing and more people are signing up to services such as social networks and music clouds. For public cloud users, issues such as privacy and security are now less of a concern. Businesses are also seeing the benefits of cloud computing in the form of reduced operational costs and increased processing power. Just as the Internet revolutionized computing in the 1990s, cloud computing may be the next great computer revolution.

GLOSSARY

app short for applications software, or a program that tells a computer or other electronic device to do something

clients computer hardware or software that accesses a service made available by a server

clones identical copies of something

data information

email short for electronic mail, or messages sent and received using computers and smartphones

Ethernet a system to connect computers to form a local area network with protocols that control the flow of information

Graphical User Interface (GUI) a visual way of interacting with a computer using icons, menus, and windows

hard drive the parts of an electronic device that store information

hardware the physical parts of a computer system, such as the machines and the cables that connect them

integrated circuit an electronic circuit formed on a semiconducting material

interface the point where two systems meet and interact

Internet the network of smaller computer networks that join together to form a single global network

IP address short for Internet Protocol address, which is the unique string of numbers used to identify a computer on the Internet

microprocessor an integrated circuit that has all the functions to control a computer

modem a device that allows computers to send and receive information over the telephone network

MP3 a digital file format used for music

network a system of interconnected computers

operating systems programs that control how computers work

playlist a list of recorded music

router a device that forwards data packets through a computer network

servers supercomputers designed for a specific task, for example, storing information or running a network

smartphones cell phones that have some of the features of personal computers, such as Internet access

software a computer application or program designed to do a specific task, for example, send email, edit photos, or record music

tablet a small, portable computer contained within a flat screen, such as an iPad

tweets short 140-character messages posted on the social networking site Twitter

upload to post images and other computer files on the Internet

WiFi a system that allows computers and cell phones to connect to computer networks without a traditional system of cables

FOR MORE INFORMATION

Books

Rodriguez, L. Phillipe. *All About Computers*. Bloomington, IN: Author House, 2012.

Rooney, Anne. *Great Big Book of Computing*. London, UK: QED Publishing, 2010.

Swanson, Jennifer. *How the Internet Works*. North Mankato, MN: The Child's World, 2011.

Websites

Watch a short video clip about cloud computing at:
www.whiteboardadvisors.com/news/kids-explain-cloud-computing

Find out about Apple Computer's cloud service, iCloud, at:
www.apple.com/icloud

The popular How Stuff Works website explains the technology behind cloud computing at:
www.howstuffworks.com/cloud-computing/cloud-computing.htm

INDEX

ML   12-14